D1458096

CHINA
EVERYDAY!

ZHANG YAO
BU YI

PAGE ONE

CHINA EVERYDAY
Copyright © 2007 PAGE ONE PUBLISHING PRIVATE LIMITED

First published in 2007 by:
Page One Publishing Private Limited
20 Kaki Bukit View
Kaki Bukit Techpark II
Singapore 415956
Tel: (65) 6742-2088
Fax: (65) 6744-2088
enquiries@pageonegroup.com
www.pageonegroup.com

Distributed by:
Page One Publishing Private Limited
20 Kaki Bukit View
Kaki Bukit Techpark II
Singapore 415956
Tel: (65) 6742-2088
Fax: (65) 6744-2088

Editorial Director: Kelley Cheng
Authors: Zhang Yao & Bu Yi
Sub-Editor: Elaine Lee
Design & Layout: Beverly Chong
Photographers: Zhang Yao & Bu Yi

ISBN 978-981-245-330-3

All rights reserved. No part of this publication may be reproduced, stored in any
retrieval system or transmitted, in any form or by any means, electronic, mechani-
cal, photocopying, recording or otherwise, without prior permission in writing
from the publisher. For information, contact Page One Publishing Private Limited,
20 Kaki Bukit View, Kaki Bukit Techpark II, Singapore 415956.

Printed and bound in China.

contents

The 1.3 billionth Chinese was born on a Thursday morning in Beijing. Just two minutes after midnight, a boy of 3.66 kilograms drew his first breath and uttered his first cries at the Beijing Hospital of Gynaecology and Obstetrics. It has been 10 years since the 1.2 billionth baby was born in China, a full decade for another 100 million people to be born in this country and a sign that population growth has slowed

down. According to the 2000 national census, the percentage of people aged 65 and older has already reached 6.96 per cent, and this is estimated at increasing to 11.8 per cent by 2020. Wang Guo Qiang, deputy director of the National Population and Family Planning Commission of China, observed, "1.3 billion is a vast number. It will put great pressure on the economy, society, resources and the environment."

圖案

GRAPHIC AND
DESIGN ELEMENTS

Traditional Chinese graphic designs, illustrations and typography embody distinctive symbolic meaning. The dragon and the phoenix when placed together is symbolic of double happiness, as with the propitious cloud, the plum flower, even the colour red are emblematic in their meaning. The openings in garden walls within traditional Chinese homes, commonly called *moon gates*, are fashioned in an assortment of shapes,

from geometric shapes like the hexagon, octagon or rectangle; to fancy shapes of the gourd and palm leaf, each representing specific aspirations of the owner. The gates serve multi-purposes apart from forming the threshold to the boundary walls. When peeped through, the *moon gate* gives glimpses of the landscape, creating sequential framing of the scenic views beyond the walls and create depth in perception.

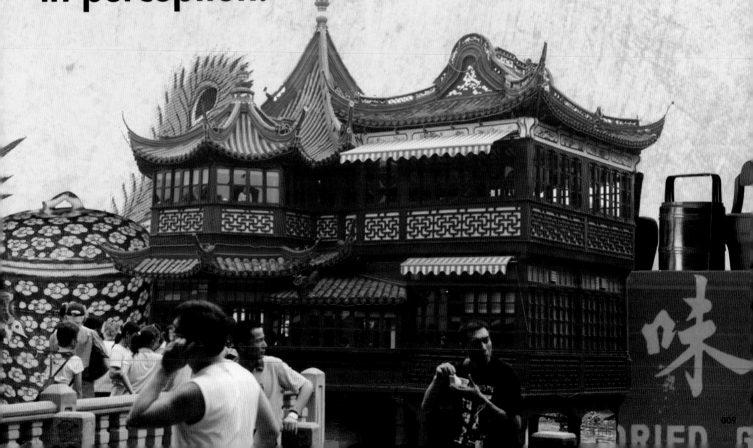

Double Happiness

The Chinese character *xi* (喜), for happiness, is customarily printed or cut on red paper, doubled (囍), and strategically placed within the sight of a young bride or groom. The story goes that in ancient Tang Dynasty, there was a student, who was making his way to the capital for the imperial examinations. Unfortunately, he fell ill on route as he was passing through a mountain village. The young man, under the care of a herbal doctor and his kind daughter, got well soon. By the time he had to leave, the young man and the girl had fallen in love. The young man excelled in the examinations and picked up the first prize, and was ensured a promising future as an official. The young man and the girl soon got married. During the wedding, the couple doubled the Chinese character xi and hung them on the wall. From then on it became an auspicious practice for newly-weds to use the double happiness character.

DRAGON

The dragon is a key design symbol throughout Chinese history. The original form of the Chinese dragon, as an ancient totem, guardian god and source of rain, appeared around 3000 BC, when the primitive Chinese society was at its demise and the historical era of Chinese civilization beginning to emerge. The Chinese consider themselves descendents of the dragon. This divine creature combines features of animals such as antlers of the deer, mane of the horse, ears of the ox, neck of the snake, claws of the eagle, soles of the tiger and scales of the fish. It is often accompanied by motifs of clouds, thunder, wind and rain. According to Chinese legend, this mythical creature can wilfully fly in the air, swim in the water and even walk on land. The dragon is so representative of celestial and terrestrial power, Chinese emperors proclaimed themselves as its incarnations to consolidate superior dominance. Throughout the long Chinese feudal history, the dragon represented the throne and the royal authority, gradually becoming the principal decorative element of imperial architecture, clothing and fixtures around the palace. Similar terms evolved, like *dragon seat* for the throne, *dragon robe* for the gown of the emperor and *dragon bed* where he sleeps. The dragon represents the masculine, where the phoenix epitomises the feminine.

Phoenix

As the symbol of high virtue, feminine grace and prosperity, the phoenix represents the Chinese empress. Like the dragon, the Chinese phoenix is also a fictitious creature. It first appeared in China around 2600 BC. According to Chinese mythology, the sky was divided into four quadrants - east, west, north and south – respectively guarded by the four celestial creatures dragon, unicorn, tortoise and phoenix. The phoenix ruled over the southern quadrant, representing the sun with its distinct bright red colour, which gave the phoenix its name *vermilion bird*. As the sovereign of the bird species, the phoenix has the head of a pheasant, beak of the parrot, body of the mandarin duck, wings of the roe, plumage of the peacock and legs of the crane. It also incorporates features like neck of the snake, back of the tortoise and tail of the fish. In the prevalent Buddhist tale, the phoenix is reborn in the fire to regain eternal life.

Auspicious subjects form important design elements for the Chinese. Flowers, birds and fishes are some of the rich graphic elements depicting joyous themes in Chinese tales and myths. Other auspicious subjects the Chinese favour are eternal wishes of happiness, prosperity and longevity.

福
Luck

The Chinese God of Luck is usually dressed in blue. Fu Xing, the Star of Fortune and Luck, is the deity to pray to for Heaven's favour and protection. He is frequently connected with Tian Guan, the Ruler of Heaven.

禄
Prosperity

The God of Prosperity, Lu Xing, is the Star of Honour and Status. The Chinese character lu originally refers to rewards for high-ranking court officials, eventually evolved to become the symbol for a successful career. Sharing the same sound is the Chinese character *lu*, for deer, frequently depicted in traditional graphics.

壽
Longevity

The God of Longevity, Shou Xing, is the Star of Longevity. The distinctive deity has a baldhead with an enormously high forehead and white eyebrows. He holds the peach of immortality in his hand and is often symbolically represented by a mushroom or a turtle.

帝
Emperor

The Chinese emperors considered themselves incarnations of real dragons and the sons of God. They are expected to live for ten thousand years.

王
Aristocracy

Unlike their Western counterparts, Chinese aristocracy were not entitled to possess territories. Aristocracy was a title indicating their noble birth or extraordinary achievements.

將
General

The general refers to a high rank army officer or the military commander in the Chinese army. In ancient China, it was one of the two career aspirations of well-educated and able-bodied young men.

相
Prime Minister

The prime minister is the head of the imperial cabinet. Historically, Chinese officials were enlisted from imperial examinations. As the principal official, the prime minister possessed intelligence with the highest of morals.

GOD OF THE GATE

The God of the Gate is one of the most illustrated deities in Chinese folk art. Originating around the time of the Han Dynasty, the custom of pining up images of a God of the Gate is still practised extensively today. Historical characters revered for their sense of loyalty, piety, and justice, are immotalised as Gods of the Gate. Guan Gong, Yue Fei, Zhu Ge Liang, Zheng Cheng Gong and Liang Hong Yu are favourite figures. Commonly associated with the Dragon Boat Festival, the image of Zhong Kui, the ghost-catcher is believed to ward off spirits following the ceremonies of sacrifice to the God of Kitchen.

門神
GOD OF THE GATE

諸葛
ZHUGE LIANG OR KONGMING

The Prime Minister of Shu state (Ad 221-263), whose name is synonymous with wisdom in China.

鍾馗
ZHONG KUI

好好學習，天天向上

HONOUR THE PARENTS.
BE POLITE TO THE GUEST.
EARLY TO BED.
RESPECT THE ELDERLY

WASH THE HANDS BEFORE MEALS.
RISE EARLY TO FACE THE SUN.
NO ONE POCKETS ANYTHING FOUND ON THE ROAD.

招財童子

AN ABUNDANT HARVEST OF GRAIN.

HARMONIOUS IMMORTALS BRING HAPPINESS TO NEWLY-WEDS.

A BEAUTIFUL IMMORTAL BRINGS THE BABY.

The Three Character Primer is a collection of three-word sentences. Like a poem, four such sentences make a part. Wang Yin Ling wrote the Three Character Primer during Song Dynasty. In ancient times, children as young as three or four years old had to recite all the primers, as the basic rules to humanity.

Three Character Primer

Of old, the mother of Mencius
chose a neighbourhood
and when her child would not
learn,
she broke the shuttle from the
loom.

Tou of the Swallow Hills
had the right method
He taugh five son,
each of whom raised the family
reputation.

To feed without teaching,
is the father's fault.
To teach without severity,
is the teacher's laziness.

If the child does not learn,
this is not as it should be.
If he does not learn while young,
what will he be when old ?

If jade is not polished,
it cannot become a thing of use.
If a man does not learn,
he cannot know his duty towards
his neighbour.

三字經

Family Happiness

The traditional Chinese family, *jia* (家), advocate patrilinear, patriarchical and virilocal concepts. The patrilinear family name and heritage were perpetuated mainly through male descendants. In hierarchy, the patriarchical family is organized with prime authority in the hands of the most senior male. The virilocal mentality also prefers and expects newly-weds to live with the groom's family. Chinese families advocate sharing a common household to form a kinship of extended families, formed by members who are related genealogically, either by common ancestors or by marriage.

A patriarch and his wife head the traditional Chinese family. Their household should auspiciously include five sons, with wives and children, who are in turn grown adults with wives. The family excluded daughters who were married and became members of other families.

In traditional Chinese families, the hierarchal order was so strong no two members were equal in authority. Senior generations were superior to junior generations, older members were superior to younger ones, and men were superior to women. Unlike Western concepts of individuality, members in the Chinese family address each other by their relationship.

Previous page on the left:
The ideal Chinese family has three, four, even five generations living in the same household with many sons and their wives, and lots of grandchildren.

Previous page on the right:
A really happy family should also be prosperous. To gain fortune is the wish of every family. Especially during the Chinese New Year celebrations, families hang all kinds of auspicious pictures to pray for wealth and health.

女人角色

Role of the Chinese Woman

The ancient Chinese woman followed the dictums of the Three Obediences and Four Virtues. When single, they obeyed the father, when married the husband and later the son. Traditionally, women were expected to bear many children, the more the merrier, especially if the children were male. Moreover, the virtuous woman should be a pillar of the household, as successful husbands were mostly not at home.

Title brings honour to ancestors and supports a luxurious lifestyle. If a member of the family was highly ranked, even their domestic animals enjoy higher status. Hence, in ancient China, the role of a wife is predominantly to support the husband building a career, and school their sons in preparation of their imperial exams so that they too may enjoy a smooth career.

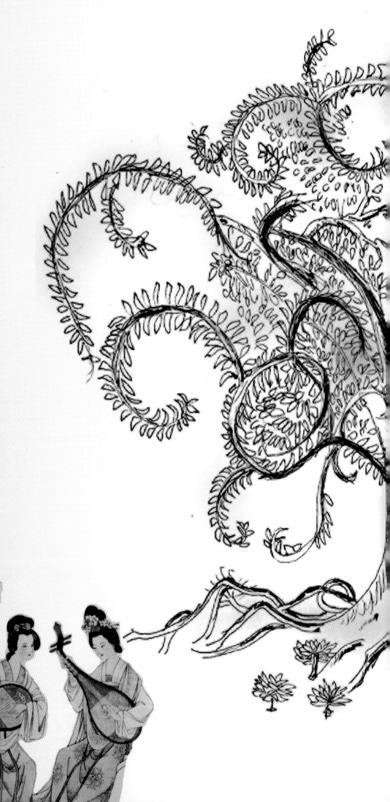

To help the husband being promoted to a higher office and rank

A pretty woman and her children with bright future. In ancient China, it is prefered to have more children, particularly the child is a boy.

Show filial piety to the parents.

神仙美女

The four most beautiful women in ancient China, Xi Shi, Wang Zhao Jun, Diao Chan and Yang Gui Fei possessed the most astounding elegance. They metaphorically made fish sink (沈魚), wild geese fall from mid-flight (落雁) shut the moonlight off (閉月), and shamed the flowers (羞花). Their beauty formed the benchmark for the classic Chinese beauty

The traditional Chinese aesthetics for beauty included a melon-seed-shaped face (瓜子脸), defined with willow-leaf-shaped eyebrows (柳叶眉), almond-shaped eye (杏仁眼), tiny red-cherry-like mouth (樱桃小口), full and oval ears long and had slim, jade-like hands (玉手).

清末国年
民初

Turn of Century

Towards the end of the Qing Dynasty, at the beginning of the Republic era, the introduction of Western concepts influenced women, who still maintained the traditional stereotypes of their roles in society and at home. Women began to follow new Western trends acceptable to the Chinese society. They played the violin, took up foreign languages and raised dogs, though they still had bound feet.

Shanghai Lady

Western lithography, introducing the necessary printing know-how to China in the late 1800s, made the trend of Shanghai posters possible. Their popularity took off in the 1920s, when foreign companies began using attractive women at leisure, in trendy fashion or even scantily clad as main themes for their posters.

This potpourri of themes, ideas and techniques created what is identifiable today as Chinese calendar posters or Chinese lady posters. The posters ushered a new trendy lifestyle for the Chinese.

01 In old Shanghai, a woman who smoked was considered very trendy.

02 Western goods entered the Chinese market during the early Republican period, influencing fashion and local culture. The model in this advertisement wore clothes distinctive of the era.

03 An advertisement of Art Publishing House even shows nudes in public.

03

Just before the Japanese war broke out, there were more than 70 artists involved in making posters. The largest studio in Shanghai, Zhi Ying Studio, produced more than 80 works a year during this busy period. Modelled by famous movie stars and singers, these vintage Chinese posters are wonderful examples of how Eastern and Western cultural influences met and merged in Shanghai.

01 A Chinese girl in a *qi pao* dress, smiles like a Hollywood star.

02 Vintage Chinese posters, reveals the curious mixture of Eastern themes with Western cultural influences and painting techniques.

03 Another poster illustrating the popular mixture of Chinese with Western styles.

04 With the increased popularity of Western goods, advertisements of foreign wines and cigarette flood the Chinese market.

02

03

01

01

艺术片

本片根据巴金同名小说改编
通过一个旧家庭的分化与没落，映
现了当时中国社会的复杂面貌。

上海电影制片厂出品 中国电影发行公司发行

02

反特侦探故事片，我公安
侦破敌人的阴谋疑心，取得信任
扮前侦察活动，侦查故事片。

惊险故事片

03

编剧 蓝琴 导演 冼群

女司机

中央电影局上海电影制片厂出品

革命電影海報
1950-1960

04

05

春之歌

彩色故事片

红色娘子军

彩色艺术片

01 The poster of the 1956 film Family, adapted from the same name novel by Ba Jin, a famous Chinese author.

02 An anti-espionage film On the Spy's Track into Tiger Den, 1956.

03 Woman Driver was a 1950 film reflecting the image of the new woman of communist China.

04 The Song of Youth, film poster, 1959.

05 Poster for a 1960 revolution film, Red Woman Detachment.

Poster art in China did not die out with the arrival of the new communist government in autumn 1949, although it took a radical shift. Following the days of the revolution and the founding of Red China in the 1950s, poster styles catered political needs and often in distinctive red. During the early days of revolution, posters still advertised goods and services, though the designs took on a new flavour. Images of women stopped being attractive or erotic, the robust worker and leftist students, even female soldiers became the new idols.

01

02

无 产 阶 级 专 政 万 岁

03

04

The Great Cultural Revolution, which lasted from May 1966 to October 1976, is one of the most turbulent movements in Chinese history. During this period, the graphic style and content focused on direct propaganda purposes. Ubiquitous posters of the Red Guards became an important tool for different factions.

01 The image of women during the Great Leap Forward, a time when labour enjoyed highest glory.

02 Women rose to an equal status with men during the revolution, the Chinese saying to hold up half the sky, indicated both sexes were on par in terms of responsibilities, including the defence of their country.

03 Founder of the Soviet Union, Lenin, was idolised.

04 Model plays matured during the Cultural Revolution between 1966-1976. There were eight of them, and they were the only plays performed at that time. This image shows a scene from the model play, Take Over of Wei-Hu Mountain.

05 A popular memorabilia from the Cultural Revolution features quotations of Chairman Mao Ze Dong on the front and a calendar on the back.

毛主席语录

革命的思想斗争和艺术斗争，必须服从于政治的斗争，因为只有经过政治，阶级和群众的需要才能集中地表现出来。

《在延安文艺座谈会上的讲话》

05

Great Cultural Revolution 1966-76

MATCHBOX LABELS FROM EARLY TIMES OF REPUBLIC CHINA

火花

MATCHBOX LABELS

Originally, paper labels were affixed on matchboxes to distinguish the various match brands. Gradually, messages were designed on matchbox labels and they became a source of information. The variations in design attracted collectors. Today, there is even the term phillumeny for matchbox labels collecting.

Chinese *flower and bird patterns* are design elements commonly employed for their symbolic meanings. Contrary to its term, *flower and bird patterns* include flora and fauna like bamboo, orchids and plum blossoms, insects, fish and animals. Derived from their natural characteristic, each element embodies its own symbolic meaning. Common elements include the bamboo for uprightness; the lotus for purity and the plum blossom with its ability to withstand the severe winter cold is for courage and perseverance. Birds are often considered as heavenly spirits, signs of freedom and longevity, sometimes even as soul of a deceased person. Other than in paintings, *flower and bird patterns* are also used in decoration for their metaphorical and allegorical meaning.

花鳥

FLOWERS AND BIRDS

窗子圖案

PANE DESIGN

Traditional Chinese houses are often decorated with carved windows covered with rice paper. The carvings, inspired from plants like the plum blossom, diffuse natural light entering the room, creating a serene and peaceful atmosphere. Throughout the day as the light changes, so will the atmosphere. Geometric motifs like the shape of coins are also featured on windowpane. The repetitive effects of the pane pattern create a relaxing retreat from the rest of the world.

門框圖案

DOOR FRAMES SIGN

In China, philosophical concepts like – the sky and man are one – can be seen from the terming of important architectural elements like the door. Expressed like the face of a man, the lintel is called the *forehead* and the vertical doorframes *cheek*.

剪紙圖案

Papercut design

Paper-cutting is a form of folk paper art popularised by the Chinese. Paper-cuttings are pasted on windows as ornaments. In the northern part of China, the windows of farmhouses are framed by wooden lattices of geometric patterns, with a layer of white leather paper pasted on. During important holidays such as the Festival of Spring, the old leather paper is replaced with new paper-cuttings to signify the welcoming of a New Year. Flora and fauna figurines and theatrical tales were popular themes of window paper-cuttings.

Douxiang Paper-Cutting

Dou Xiang paper-cuttings are used as decorations during sacrificing rituals. These cuttings of mythical themes, including spirits and other legendary characters, are usually engraved on wax-polished paper.

Gate Label

Gate labels are paper-cuttings that are hung on gate sills. They are also called the hanging label or hanging money for the semblance and are usually embedded with figures of flowers, phoenix, dragons, and other auspicious characters. Gate labels are hung as a series of a flags engraved on red or multi-coloured paper, with geometrical shapes.

Festive Paper-Cutting

Cuttings adorn household appliances and furniture such as teapots, soapboxes, basins and dressing mirrors during the festive seasons. The red colour and auspicious themes imply happiness. These festive paper-cuttings appear in the form of circles, rectangles, peaches, pomegranates and other auspicious shapes.

京劇臉譜

Opera facial painting

The masks represent the roles of the characters in Chinese opera. For example, a red face usually depicts the role's bravery, righteousness and loyalty; a white face symbolises a sinister role's treachery and guile; and a green face describes mainly stubbornness, impulsiveness and a lack of self-restraint.

In addition, the patterns of the facial painting also reveal more information about the role. Without a word, the unique make-up of the opera allows the characters on the stage to reveal themselves to the audience.

Beijing opera, more commonly known as Peking opera to westerners, is deemed the national opera of China. The accompanying music, singing and costumes are full of Chinese cultural facts. Engaging plots unfolding, beautiful facial paintings, exquisite costumes, graceful gestures and acrobatic fighting are all underlined by the most exotic singing.

There are four main roles in Beijing Opera: *Sheng, Dan, Jing and Chou.*
Sheng refers to the leading male actor.
Dan is the female role, also played by men in the past.
Jing is the face-painted role that represents a warrior, hero, statesman, adventurer or demon, and is mostly played by a male.
Chou refers to a clown who is characterised by a white patch on the nose.

食物
FOOD

Eating is a major affair for all Chinese, many regard eating as a form of art – a comprehensive combination of sight, smell, touch, taste and even sound. Delicious and nutritious food is highly regarded among the basics of ordinary life. Restaurants offer menus with hundreds of dishes, more choices than the wine lists of most sophisticated restaurants in the Western world. Each day starts with the morning market. To buy food in the morning market is a matter of cardinal importance to a Chinese family. In the past, the morning markets were all outdoors and scattered around town, but now more and more markets take place in sheltered market halls. The open-air markets are rather local, most of the

hawkers are suburban peasants who pick the fresh vegetables in the morning and feed the fowls with rice and vegetables. The customers of the morning markets live nearby, so some of them will just wear pyjamas because they fear that the freshest foods will be sold quickly, so they go to the food markets right after waking up. The morning markets are lively, the air filled with hawkers shouting, voices bargaining, greetings exchanged between friends as well as noises made by the fowls....

Dim Sum

In the southern part of China and Hong Kong, *yam cha* - literally meaning *drink tea* - is the Cantonese-style breakfast of indulgent feasting on countless snacks that make the envy of every gourmet. Served also as lunch or brunch, a mind-boggling variety of choices of *dim sum* snacks are accompanied by a pot of strong and often pitch black tea.

Such meals sometimes take several hours, lasting from morning till early afternoon with family or friends in relatively noisy and packed restaurants.

Dim sum is a Cantonese term for small snacks, including different styles of buns like *bao zi*, turnip cakes, lotus leaf rice, semi-transparent *shui jiao* style dumplings, taro root dumplings and rice rolls, some of which would be filled with a wide variety of ingredients including beef, chicken, pork, prawns and vegetarian options. Many *dim sum* restaurants also offer plates of steamed or stir-fried green vegetables, roasted meats, congee porridge and other soups.

Dim sum is prepared by traditional cooking methods like steaming, frying, baking, stewing and simmering. The portion of *dim sum* snacks is usually small, like a mouthful and normally served in three or four servings per dish. Because of the small portions, everybody can try a wide variety of food.

Dim sum dishes can be ordered from a menu or by pointing to the trolleys on which waiters wheel around. Traditionally, the cost of the meal is calculated based on the number and size of dishes left on the patron's table or through the number of snack stamps on your card.

Rice

Rice and flour are the two main traditional staples in China. Generally speaking in the southern part of China, the area of rice farming, people like to eat cooked rice. And up North, the area of wheat farming, people like to eat noodles, dumplings, steamed buns and pancake-like bread.

无锡米
无水
5
锡米

Noodles

They can be purchased dry or fresh and in a variety of shapes, sizes and textures. Noodles can be served in soups and casseroles, fried or with toppings. According to Chinese tradition, noodles are a symbol of long life and good health; therefore certain types of noodles should be served long and uncut.

Dry noodles can be stored for up to six months in a cool and dry place, but fresh noodles should be wrapped in plastic and stored in the refrigerator or freezer.

Many northern or western Chinese style noodles are still pulled by hand all over China in street stalls into la mian, which requires an impressive skill while others are cut with a small knife from a solid piece of dough directly into the boiling water.

中國菜

Chinese Regional Cuisines

Chinese cuisine has a number of different styles, but the most influential and typical known by the public are the Four Cuisines, namely: Shandong cuisine, Sichuan cuisine, Guangdong cuisine and Jiangsu cuisine. The essential factors that establish a style are complex and include history, cooking features, geography, climate, resources and lifestyle. Cuisines from different regions are so distinctive that sometimes despite the fact that two areas are geographically neighbours, their cooking styles may differ completely.

Shandong Cuisine

This is the local flavour of Jinan city and Jiaodong peninsula, which derived from the use of shallots and garlic. Both restaurant chefs and family cooks are experts at cooking seafood, soup, meat and fowl. The recipes are those that once delighted the royal court and were served to the emperor.

Guangdong Cuisine

Guangdong cuisine holds fine and rare ingredients in high regard, and is prepared with polished skills and in a dainty style. It emphasises a flavour that is clear but not light, refreshing but not common and tender but not crude.

Sichuan Cuisine

Sichuan cuisine is a combination of Chengdu and Chongqing traditional cooking styles. From as early as the Qing Dynasty, 1644 - 1911, books have systematically recorded a total of 38 cooking methods including scalding, wrapping, baking, mixing, stewing, to name a few. Apart from the *Seven Taste* of sweet, sour, tingling, spicy, bitter, piquant and salty, Sichuan cuisine is defined by aromas that include the *Eight Flavours* of sour with spice, tingling with pepper, tingling with spice, red spicy oily, fish flavoured, odd flavoured, ginger flavoured, and even the flavour of home cooking. Potent seasoning is featured such as the *Three Peppers*, consisting of Chinese prickly ash, pepper and hot pepper and the *Three Aromas* referring to the shallot, ginger and garlic. Sichuan style spicy flavours typically leave a tingling feeling on the tongue.

Jiangsu Cuisine

Jiangsu cuisine is developed from the local recipes of Yangzhou, Suzhou and Nanjing. Its main cooking techniques are braising and stewing, thereby enhancing the original light flavour and sauce. The elegant colours and pleasant combination of salty and sweet tastes will soothe your stomach. Jiangsu cuisine has several branches including Shanghai cuisine; Nanjing cuisine, which is known for its duck recipes; and Suxi cuisine with its floral hues, generally recognisable by a light and sweet taste.

北京烤鴨

Beijing Roast Duck

Beijing roast duck is thought to be amongst the most delicious dishes in China, but is certainly not the lightest one. There are two different ways of roasting a duck. One uses a closed oven and straw as fuel, which prevents the flames from touching the duck. Before being put into the oven, the duck is marinated and stuffed with gravy to roast the duck on its outside and braise its inside at the same time.

The other uses an oven without a door. After spreading a dressing all over the duck, it will be hung in the oven above the flames created from the burning of fruit-tree wood, cooking it in forty minutes.

When roasted and dried, the duck will look brilliantly dark red, shiny with oil, and have a crisp skin and tender meat. Hence before cutting it, the chef will first display the entire duck at the table. Then, he will slice it into around 120 pieces before serving it together with special pancakes, sesame buns, green leeks and sweet sauce. Diners can wrap duck slices, leek and sauce according to their preferences in a pancake or a sesame bun and eat with their bare hands. This is one of the few times where chopsticks are not a must.

Other parts of the duck are served as either cold dishes with liver, wings, stomach, web and eggs, or hot dishes with heart, tongue and kidneys. The carcass and bones are normally removed and boiled together with Chinese watermelon and cabbage for a light duck soup after the feast.

The duck slices are rolled in thin pancakes with a dip of *tian mian jiang*, which is a sweet sauce made of fermented flour, along with leek or cucumber cut in thin strips.

大閘蟹

Hairy Crab

Hairy crab or *da zha xie* is a local delicacy found in lakes and ponds near Shanghai, with the most famous ones from Yang Cheng Lake. In autumn and winter, almost every family spends an evening with the tasty crabs at least once, as it takes patience and skilled practice to crack and peel the crusts and suck out all meat.

As a rule and despite the logistical challenges, the crabs need to be alive before being steamed and served. Even with absolutely no extra ingredients, true connoisseurs claim their tender white meat tastes very good. Crabs are usually served with vinegar and finely chopped ginger. It is said that on the Chinese Lunar calendar, the ninth month is the best time to eat female crabs while in the tenth month, the male crabs are supposed to be in their optimal taste.

Hairy crabs can be steamed or boiled. When its shell turns red, it is time to get the fingers to work on the delicacy.

北方宮廷點心

Dim Sum of Imperial Court

Beijing was the capital of four dynasties - Jin, Yuan, Ming and Qing, so the dim sum offered to the emperor was called *dim sum of imperial court* (宮廷點心).

Today, authentic Imperial style dim sum, can be tasted at Fang Shan Restaurant in Beihai Park, Beijing, founded in 1925 by the chefs of the last emperor Zhao Ren Zhai and his son Zhao Bing Nan. Their specialty dim sum includes *Sweet Yellow Pea*, *Rocking Donkey* and *Chilled Apple-Crab Cake*.

The imperial treatment can also be experienced at Bai Jia Da Zhai Men near Zhong Guan Cun in Beijing. Bai Jia Da Zhai Men is the former residence of a Prince, which adjoins an impressive Chinese garden. Waitresses of the restaurant serve in period costumes.

Jiao zi is a Chinese ravioli-like dumpling that consists of noodle-like dough filled with minced meat and vegetables. Other popular fillings include mix green vegetables with shrimp, ground lamb, ground pork, ground beef, and even fish, although some are only vegetarian. *Jiao zi* is usually steamed or boiled.

Prepare the dumpling filling:
Shred Chinese cabbage, sprinkle with salt and then squeeze out excess liquid after chopping finely. Shred leeks, fresh shitake mushrooms, shrimp and ginger. Mix the ground pork with the seasoning. Add vegetables and mix well.

Making the dumpling skin:
Mix flour with a pinch of salt in a bowl. Pour lukewarm water over the flour mixture bit by bit while mixing well. Knead dough by hand until smooth, stretchy and shiny. Form a ball and cover with a wet cloth for 30 minutes. Divide dough into several smaller rolls to be cut into small individual pieces. Roll those out to 6 cm circles with a rolling pin, thinning out at the edges.

Make the dumplings:
Place a small amount of filling in the centre of dumpling skin and close the skin around the filling. Place filled skins on a plate with a drop of oil to prevent skins from sticking.

Cook the dumplings and serve:
Place the dumplings into boiling water and after the second boil, add 1 cup of cold water and cover briefly. Repeat this step again and when the water reaches the third boil, the dumplings are done and can be served directly without soup. Some people dip one end of the dumpling into a vinegar-soy sauce mixture while northern Chinese eat them with garlic.

水餃

Dumpling

中國老酒

Chinese Wines

Chinese liquor and yellow wine are famous spirits from China.

Chinese liquor is crystal clear, aromatic and tasty. Made from various staples like broomcorn, corn, rice and wheat, it contains a staggering 60% alcohol. Chinese liquor is believed to date back to the Song Dynasty, 960-1297. The most famous brand is Mao Tai, which is known as the *national liquor*. Other excellent brands include Du Kang, Wu Liang Ye and Lu Zhou Te Qu. The favourite of the Chinese is the Er Guo Tou by Red Star.

Yellow wine is a traditional rice wine with a history of 5,000 years and unique to China. Made from rice and sticky rice, it is renowned for its yellow colour and lustre. After the fermentation process, the wine has a balmy fragrance and is sweet tasting with little or no sharpness. It ranges between 10 and 15% alcohol content. The most popular brands of yellow wine come from Shaoxing in Zhejiang Province, called Shaoxing Lao Jiu or Shaoxing Hua Diao. There is also the common yellow wine, Te Jia Fan that is more affordable and suitable as a cooking wine.

Tea

With thousands of years of tea culture, China is the homeland of tea. Chinese tea is classified into five categories according to the different methods of processing. One of the most popular is green tea, which keeps its original leaf colour and does not ferment during processing. *Long jing cha* or *dragon well tea* is one of the best and lightest green tea in China.

A new tea plant usually grows for five years before its leaves can be picked. Within 30 years, the trunk of the old plant must be cut off to force new stems to grow out of the roots in the coming year. By repeating rejuvenation in this way, a plant may serve for about 100 years.

The season of tea picking depends on the local climate and varies from area to area. The picking of *long jing cha,* usually starts from the end of March and lasts through October. A plant is picked 20 to 30 times at intervals no longer than seven to ten days before the quality of tea deteriorates.

New leaves are parched in tea cauldrons manually even until today. Tea cauldrons are heated electrically to a temperature of about 25°C. It takes four pounds of fresh leaves to produce one pound of parched tea.

Food stores in China are big market places selling processed foods and all kinds of produce from all over the country. Especially with the approach of the Chinese New Year and other festivals, the crowds flock to the food store to buy specialty produces.

Under communist rule, there were more than ten food stores in Shanghai, all ranked and named accordingly by grade. Nowadays, with the increasing popularity of supermarkets, the food store no longer plays such an important part in the daily life of the Chinese.

食品店
FOODSTORES

The grade-one food store in Shanghai is found on Nanjing Road. It is the largest of its kind in the city and popular with visitors to Shanghai, who visit to buy Chinese specialties. To the locals, this store is their first choice for local and specialty produces.

关东芝麻糖
一律10元每斤

零食

Snacks

Melon seeds are a simple and affordable snack. The dry roasted seeds with inedible crispy shells and delicious kernels are skilfully split open on the front teeth to extract the kernels. Snacks of leisure suitable for anytime of the day, melon seeds are associated with relaxed times and festive seasons. There are various kinds of melon seeds, such as watermelon seeds and pumpkin seeds, in natural or salted flavours. Sunflower seeds, though not in the melon category, are also prepared similarly and have become a favourite.

The Chinese enjoy their tea with snacks like melon seeds, nuts, plums, waxberry, dried fruit, candy and cakes, to name a few favoured choices.

Household Items

家庭用品

木與藤器
wood and vine ware

A wooden basket without handle, painted with red lacquer, is usually used to store rice or other dry food.

wood ware painted with lacquer, were used as container for food for convenience, some of them include a handle for carrying. Today wood ware is used more as decorative wedding gifts than for food storage.

Before the advent of plastics and Tupperware, wood ware is a key material next to bamboo in Chinese households. Together, they form part of a long and sophisticated tradition in the domestic realm.

Its applications range from buckets, wooden pails, rice ware, water basins, stools, pen pots, fruit bowls to even soil buckets - some of which were in beautiful shapes, covered with delicate lacquer.

Utensils made of vine strips were also an important part of the Chinese household.

083

Bamboo baskets were the most widely used daily household item, before
the introduction of plastic bags.

竹器

bamboo ware

Bamboo is not only a key material for household goods, but also more importantly a characteristic symbol of Chinese culture. Scholars favoured making the analogy between a noble man and bamboo, where its firm joints forms a rigid structure to its hollow core. Bamboo is knitted, carved and roasted to different shape for furniture and daily utensils create simple, fresh and refined living environments.

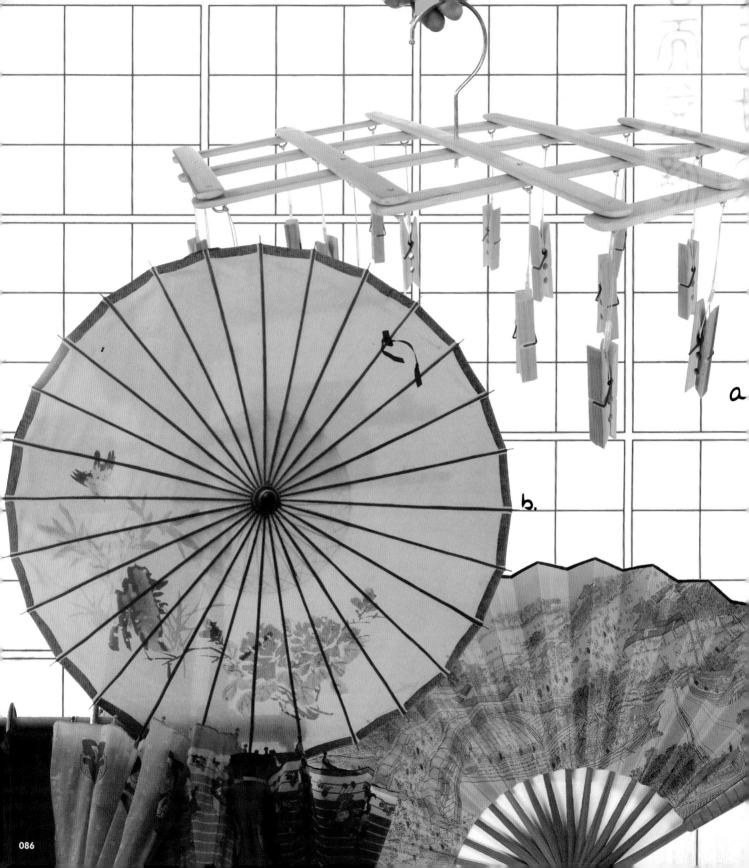

a

b.

a. This criss-crossed clothes rack made of bamboo used to be en vogue until it is almost completely replaced by its modern plastic cousin in the major cities.

b. In the Suzhou region, traditional handmade paper umbrellas are still pasted on bamboo frames.

c. The framework of handheld folding fans is normally made of bamboo. The story goes that the first folding fan was a tribute offered by the Korean envoy during the Northern Song Dynasty over a thousand years ago. Folding fans were not only a handy tool, it was popular amongst literati of ancient times to paint on the surface of the fan and even send fans to each other.

c.

日常用品

Daily Appliances

Appliances used on a day-to-day basis by the Chinese serve the functional purpose of cultivating habits and practices unique to their routine, culture, and lifestyle.

Bamboo sieves are used in the preparation of dumplings. Flour is sprinkled on the sieves and dumplings are laid out just before they are ready for cooking in boiling water.

A traditional wok is used to fry noodles and long bamboo chopsticks are used to serve the noodles.

Typical Chinese kitchen knives and cleavers are made of steel with a wooden handle. The head is rounded for leverage and the bottom is flat.

Aluminum kettles are used by the Chinese to boil water. It is common to sit these kettles on small portable stoves, fuelled by briquettes that are specially fit with holes for convenient handling with long scissor-like pincers.

Thermos bottles have moved on from aluminum to colorful plastic hulls.

Washboards of ridged wood or corrugated zinc were used until recently. Clothes are scrubbed on the ribbed surface during washing. They are still seen in the countryside today.

Stinky soap, nick-named by the Shanghainese, is a simple, perfume-free soap with high-alkaline content. It is used for washing clothes and has a long history in China.

Decorative items line the side table of a typical drawing room in a country house. It displays household treasures like the TV set, clocks, vases and other paraphernalia. On the wall, New Year paintings and poetic couplets are displayed.

床

Bed

A cooling mat of woven bamboo strips, is used instead of bed sheets in summer. Simple toweling covers are usually enough during the hot summer months.

A pillowcase with Chinese folk art painting.

Traditional Chinese hot-water bottles, *tang po zi*, are made of copper or white sheet iron and have caps that are screwed on tightly. The original versions warmed beds with hot ashes. Today, more effective heat-resistant materials like rubber or plastics replace these portable heat dispensers. In this image, the copper *tang po zi* shows the Chinese character *fu*, for luck.

The traditional winter quilts of thick cotton or silk filling are covered in exquisite silks and satins with flowers, dragon and phoenix patterns. On the inside, white or colorful cotton sheets cover the quilts and are removed once a month for washing in winter, while the outermost silken covering is rarely washed at all.

家具
CHINESE FURNITURE

Chinese screens are carved and frequently frame a mirror in the center. In ancient China, every family had a screen at the entrance of the drawing room, some even had a stone screen in their yard, right behind the entrance gate, believed keep evil away.

The couch bed, also called the *xiang fei* bed, had its place in the reading room or in pavilions facing the garden. It offered a cool rest for female household members to nap or sip tea.

The Chinese easy chair has a tilted back with arms for resting. It even has a footrest that can be neatly tucked underneath when not in use.

The Chinese cabinet is usually made of wood and painted in black lacquer to serve both the purpose of storage as well as decoration. It is usually painted with pavilions, mountain scenes, people and other colorful patterns. Some cabinets are in stunning red lacquer with bronze lock.

OUT BACKREST OR

ARMS ON FOUR LEGS

ARE TYPICAL FOR ZHE

IIANG PROVINCE IN

EASTERN CHINA

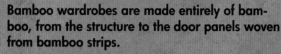

Bamboo wardrobes are made entirely of bamboo, from the structure to the door panels woven from bamboo strips.

In ancient Chinese jewelry boxes were made of rosewood and painted in red lacquer with flowers, birds, children or bamboo patterns. When opened up, the box reveals a mirror for make-up.

A small Chinese sideboard made of wood is usually painted with black lacquer. It is perfect for storage of small items, as well as for display.

Round stools on four legs, without backrest or arms are typical designs of the Zhejiang province in the eastern part of China.

Armchairs are usually of rosewood and carved with dragon patterns. Usually a marble plate adorns the middle of the backrest. The armchair is usually placed in the sitting room for guests.

The traditional Chinese lacquer plant stand is often carved with decorative patterns, with wooden struts below for added strength.

Teapot

Most Chinese tea lovers regard teapots from Yixing as the best. Yixing County, in the southern part of Jiangsu Province, has been the centre of Chinese teapot production since the Song Dynasty, 960-1279. High quality Yixing clay called *zi sha* or *purple clay* comes from the banks of Lake Tai near Nanjing. The clay has a high content of metallic oxides. Differences in kiln temperature and atmosphere create wares varying from purple to beige or green.

A good Yixing teapot pours evenly from the pot, resounds when struck and has a snugly fitted lid. The slightly absorbent pottery soaks up some of the flavour of the tea; hence it is important to drink only one kind of tea out of each teapot. Teapots with some age to them would have a distinct residue of old tea inside, which enhances the flavour of tea.

Tea plays an important role in Chinese social and spiritual life. It is a symbol of togetherness, a sharing of something enjoyable and a way of showing hospitality to visitors. It is customary for a host to fill a teacup to seven-tenths of its capacity. Saying goes that the remainder will be topped up with friendship and affection.

瓷器

Porcelain ware

Chinese porcelain is a mixture of *kaolin and petunse*, fired at a high temperature of around 1,300°C. *Kaolin* clay has such high resistance to heat, it maintains its shape during the firing, and acts as the *bone of porcelain* to the Chinese. *Petunse* on the other hand melts at high temperatures, forming a nonporous natural glass and adding translucency to porcelain. It is called the *flesh of porcelain*.

Blue and white porcelain ware is a distinct Chinese style, made popular during the Ming Dynasty. It reached its golden era of development during the reign of the Emperors Yong Le, Xuan De and Cheng Hua. Porcelain then had thick but delicate glaze and came in a wide range of shapes, designs and patterns. The glaze became lighter in colour in the later periods, and Chinese ink paintings were incorporated. During the late Ming Dynasty the blue and white porcelain enjoyed great popularity.

The Chinese abacus is a tool used to aid rapid mental calculations. The abacus has a history of thousands of years and was popularised towards the end of the Yuan Dynasty. It was taught in school during mathematic lessons and until the arrival of modern electronic calculators.

Mosquito coil incense is a traditional way to keep mosquitoes away. Li Zi Pai is one of the famous old brands in China.

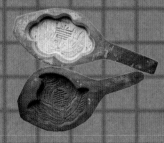

A wooden mould with a handle is used to make *mooncakes* for the Mid Autumn Festival. Carved in the middle of the moulds and impressed on the cakes are auspicious Chinese characters, such as *fu* for luck and *shou* for longevity or floral motifs.

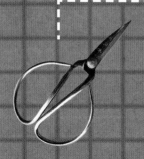

Scissors are traditionally of iron or steel, with wing-like handles. On the head of scissors, the name of its maker is engraved. One of the most famous brands in China is called Zhang Xiao Quan.

新明日用

雜

Household goods

Red plastic string is used to pack goods everywhere in China.

Portable coal stoves using specially shaped briquettes were popular in Shanghai until the 1980s. Usually made of iron, the stove has a valve under the stove. The valve controlled ventilation to the stove and could speed it up or slow it down. Opening the valve was usually the first chore children helped their parents with after school, an important task paramount to the preparation of hot water and dinner.

The *back scratch* is an extended hand used to scratch an itch on the back. The long bamboo handle with a comb head conveniently reaches round hard to get spots on the back. The handy tool featured is an-all in one. In the middle of the handle is a small abacus that functions as calculation too and doubles as massage beads. The most surprising detail of this handmade tool is the tiny *ear pick* hidden in a mini box at the end of the handle.

Wooden lacquer plates are used to display foodstuff like fruits, rice and flour.

紀念品
SOUVENIRS

Souvenirs and photos trigger memories of places visited. The variety of choices of Chinese souvenirs available is staggering, from unique keepsakes like antiques to cheap kitsch, a very popular form of Chinese memorabilia, making China the souvenir paradise for travellers. Nowadays, antiques are more often than not replicas of jade, paintings, calligraphy, cloisonné, lacquer ware and porcelain. They offer a glimpse of the profound cultural heritage.

The more recent kitsch paraphernalia available also make interesting mementos. During the time of Chairman Mao, it was fashionable in China to wear badges of his portraiture to show love and respect for the leader. Today after this era and most of its slogans have disappeared, souvenirs with Chairman Mao's portraiture mark this important epoch of China.

We must fight capitalism!

毛澤東

MAO ZEDONG

Chairman of the Chinese Communist Party, Mao Ze Dong, launched the Cultural Revolution during his last decade of power, between 1966 and 1976. Initiated to renew the spirit of the Chinese revolution, these ten years caused confusion instead to the Chinese. Memories of students as Red Guards or being sent to the countryside are immortalised in cartoons. During the period of social revolution, social activity slogans were often written on red cloth as mottos to remind of the purpose of the activity. Red became the colour that symbolises China and the revolution.

1.

2.

SIXTIES - EIGHTIES
SOUVENIRS

1. A TYPICAL CHINESE ALARM CLOCK IS ROUND, BECAUSE THE CHINESE ASSOCIATE ROUND SHAPES WITH HEAVEN AND SQUARES SYMBOLISE EARTH.

2. *BING GAN XIANG*, SIMPLE IRON BISCUIT TINS ARE PRINTED ON AND USED TO STORE BISCUITS.

3. WIND-UP MODEL PLANES WERE TO BE VERY POPULAR IN THE 1970S AND 1980S.

3.

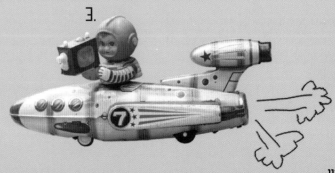

REPUBLIC PERIOD
SOUVENIRS

1. ENGAGEMENT LICENSE FROM THE 1940S WERE KEPT IN RED SCROLLS PRINTED WITH MANDARIN DUCKS, SYMBOLS OF BLISSFUL MARRIAGES.

2. PAIRS OF JARS, HAND-PAINTED WITH BUTTERFLIES AND FLOWERS, WERE OFTEN USED AS WEDDING SYMBOLS.

3. THE *HOOKAH* OR WATER PIPE IS A TRADITIONAL DEVICE FOR SMOKING. DURING THE LATE QING DYNASTY, THE WATER PIPE WAS A POPULAR DEVISE USED TO SMOKE DRY CIGARETTES.

4. BRIGHTLY DECORATED ENAMEL WASHBASINS USED TO BE VERY POPULAR IN CHINA DURING THE 1950S. AFTER THE CHINESE REVOLUTION, TYPICAL NECESSITIES PREPARED FOR NEWLYWEDS INCLUDED A SIMILAR WASHBASIN, A FOOTBATH AND A THERMOS BOTTLE.

5. CURRENCY PRINTED WITH THE PORTRAITURE OF THE PRESIDENT OF THE REPUBLIC, JIANG JIE SHI *"CHIANG KAI-SHEK"* CIRCULATED DURING THE PERIOD IN WHICH HE RULED.

6. CURRENCY PRINTED WITH THE PORTRAITURE OF SUN ZHONG SHAN *"SUN YAT-SUN"* WAS ALSO IN USE IN THE REPUBLIC OF CHINA DURING THE EARLY 20TH CENTURY.

5.

6.

REPLICATED
SOUVENIRS

1. PORCELAIN DOLLS IN ATTIRES OF THE MANCHURIAN COURT DURING THE QING DYNASTY.

2. EMPEROR QIN SHI HUANG WAS THE FIRST RULER TO UNITE CHINA. IN ORDER TO PRESERVE A MIGHTY FIGHTING CAPACITY AFTER HIS DEATH. HE ASSEMBLED AN UNDERGROUND TERRACOTTA ARMY OF NEARLY 8,000 SOLDIERS AND HORSES NEAR XIAN CITY. JUST 1.5 KM FROM HIS TOMB. THE LIFE-SIZED TERRACOTTA WARRIORS IN BATTLE ATTIRE AND FORMATION. AVERAGE 1.8M TALL. WEIGH BETWEEN 100 AND 300KG AND WERE CREATED IN A WIDE RANGE OF DIFFERENT HAIRSTYLES AND POSTURES. THE STATUES HAVE BEEN BURIED FOR MORE THAN 2,200 YEARS AND ARE CONSIDERED ONE OF THE MOST IMPORTANT ARCHEOLOGICAL DISCOVERIES OF THE 20TH CENTURY.

3. A SET OF PAINTED PORCELAIN DOLLS IN TRADITIONAL CHINESE COSTUMES.

4. REPLICAS OF SCULPTURES OF CHILDREN AT PLAY ARE POPULAR IN SOUVENIR SHOPS.

5. BEAUTIFUL WOODEN BOXES SERVED AS PILLOWS. WHICH DOUBLE UP AS CASES FOR SAFEKEEPING.

服飾

{ Clothing }

According to an old Chinese proverb, clothes maketh the man. To the Chinese, apart from ample food, having warm clothing is the most basic requirement to living. Being well fed and well dressed are regarded as signs of good fortune, beyond that would be considered a more luxurious life for the few lucky ones. In China, the aesthetics of embroidery is omnipresent and highly regarded. In fact, stunning mountain and river landscapes are usually compared to

beautiful embroidery on refined silk and brocade. There are fundamental genres of traditional Chinese clothing that form the basics of the Chinese style, like the *ao* (襖) jacket, *gua* (褂) gown, *ku* (褲) trousers, *shan* (衫) shirt, *lü* (褸) coat and *qun* (裙) skirt. Colour also plays an important symbolic role in clothing. Red, believed to bring happiness and luck, is a popular colour chosen for attires worn during the Lunar New Year and preferred choice for children, especially in the countryside.

China is the homeland of silk. Silkworm cultivation in China can be traced back at least 6,000 years. Silk production reached its peaked during the Han Dynasty, when Chinese silks were transported from Xian to Rome. The overland trade route was via the famous Silk Road. The legendary Chinese silk connected China to the rest of the world and its price once matched that of gold. The four centers of traditional silk productions are Suzhou, Hangzhou, Huzhou and Shenze, at the southern part of the Yangzi River Delta. The region is regarded as home to mulberry trees, which feed the silk worms.

Chinese Silk

Shu brocade from Sichuan originated during the Han Dynasties. Predominantly red, designs of the Shu brocade fully reflected the flowery nature of Shu culture. In the Tang Dynasty, Dou Shi Lun, the Duke of Ling Yang, created a set of designs for Shu brocade, known as the *Duke Ling Yang pattern*.

Yun brocade dates back to the Southern Dynasty and features quality material, refined weaving and the wide use of gold and silver threads. During the Yuan, Ming and Qing Dynasties, Yun brocade was a royal tribute. As modern machinery cannot replicate the unique weaving Yun Brocade considered a work of art more than fabric, remains handmade and very expensive.

Song brocade originated from the end of Northern Song Dynasty and is mainly used for framing calligraphy works. Originally used by the Ji family to frame hangings of their precious calligraphy collection. There were twenty designs to this brocade.

COTTON
Cotton

Cotton plants grow wild all over the world. China is one of the biggest cotton producers. Since 2,000 years ago, cotton plants were already cultivated in the southern and far western parts of China. The introduction of synthetic fibers in the early 1900s did not reduce the popularity of cotton. Pure cotton offers air permeability, softness and comfort. It is widely used for clothing and all kinds of domestic purposes. Today, 100% cotton not only stands for nature and purity, but also represents a high quality life style.

Indigo Print

Indigo prints are blue and white patterns printed on cotton. Technical and artistic development of indigo print reached its peak during the Song Dynasty. The Chinese use soybean, lime powder and indigo blue as dyeing color and pattern. Indigo print occupies a dominant position for Chinese people's favorite, artistic taste and best

Patterns are drawn from Chinese folklores, such as flowers, birds, legendary animals and Chinese characters. The indigo prints are for personal adornments and so on. The traditional patterns like the handkerchiefs, bed sheets, various articles for the beauty and good fortune.

唐装

Tang Suit

The *tang suit* refers to all traditional Chinese fashion. In fact, what people have over time come to define as *tang style* was created in the late Ming and early Qing Dynasty, although it referred to the prosperous Tang Dynasty. The term came about because the Chinese referred to themselves as *tang ren*, therefore the clothes they wore were called the *tang style* to distinguish themselves.

Qi pao

Qi pao or the *banner dress* is one of the most distinctive traditional dresses donned by Chinese women. Introduced by the Manchurians, who were called *banner people*, the *banner dress* was popularised in the royal court of the Qing Dynasty and with the nobility of Manchurian origin. Later, it was been gradually accepted as the typical elegant dress for Chinese women of different social strata, especially middle and upper class.

Peony is a common floral print on the clothing of Chinese ladies. It is the favourite flower of the Chinese and was chosen as the Chinese national flower. Peony stands for richness and prosperity. Peach flowers are another popular floral design favoured by Chinese ladies. It symbolises youth and vigour.

The phoenix motif was frequently used on the clothing of Chinese ladies within the Imperial Family. In Chinese mythology, the phoenix is the symbol of high virtue and grace, representing power sent from the heavens to the Empress. Empresses however often wore dragon motifs because the imperial concubines, the wives of princes and the princesses wore phoenix motifs.

The collar of the *qi pao* in the past used to be made high and tight fitting to keep warm. The idea of the high collar was not just to keep warm but also to highlight the beauty of the neck. Generally ending in a semicircle with symmetrical left and right sides, the collar stands upright to flatter the soft and slender neck of a woman. Incorporating innovations of the 20th century, one can find a wide variety of creative designs from short to long or even no collar at all. The finishing touches for the collar of a traditional *qi pao* include detailed handmade embroidery and a buttonhole loop on the collar to highlight its elegance.

The *qi pao* is generally made of silk and satin, with delicate embroidery patterns and lace borders trimmed at the collar, sleeves and hems. These fine details reveal the fine workmanship of this beautiful dress.

Nearly every colour can be used. As mentioned, the *qi pao* frequently displays traditional patterns such as Chinese dragons, different kinds of flowers, butterflies or other typical Chinese icons that are symbols for wealth and prosperity.

It is said that the *qi pao* can highlight a woman's soft curves and beauty. Like a Chinese woman's temperament, the *qi pao* is elegant and gentle, and its serenity makes a woman fascinating. A mature woman in a *qi pao* can display her graceful manner. A *qi pao* always varies with the womanly figure. For facilitate movement and a glimpse of slender legs, a *qi pao* generally has two high slits on either sides of the hem. These slits often expose more than a hint of the lady's legs when she walks. However, while a *qi pao* usually has one slit at each side of the body to facilitate movement, today you can find a variety of lengths and types of slits including one slit on the side or front only, as well *qi pao* with two slits.

旗袍

Ma Gua

馬褂

A *ma gua* is an outdoor jacket that helps keep warm. It is designed to have short, baggy sleeves and its length stays above the waist to enhance the convenience of horseback riding. Initially used by soldiers, it was called *victory gua*. *Ma gua* comes in different styles, but men are not permitted to wear a yellow *ma gua* unless they have been rewarded for something noteworthy. For a while it used to be very fashionable amongst to wealthy to wear the *ma gua* inside out, showing off leather and fur linings. From the 1930s, Western-style suits became more popular in China, especially in Shanghai. But *ma gua* is still a traditional jacket for some formal occasions. Today, *ma gua* is more popular for a wedding ceremony than a suit.

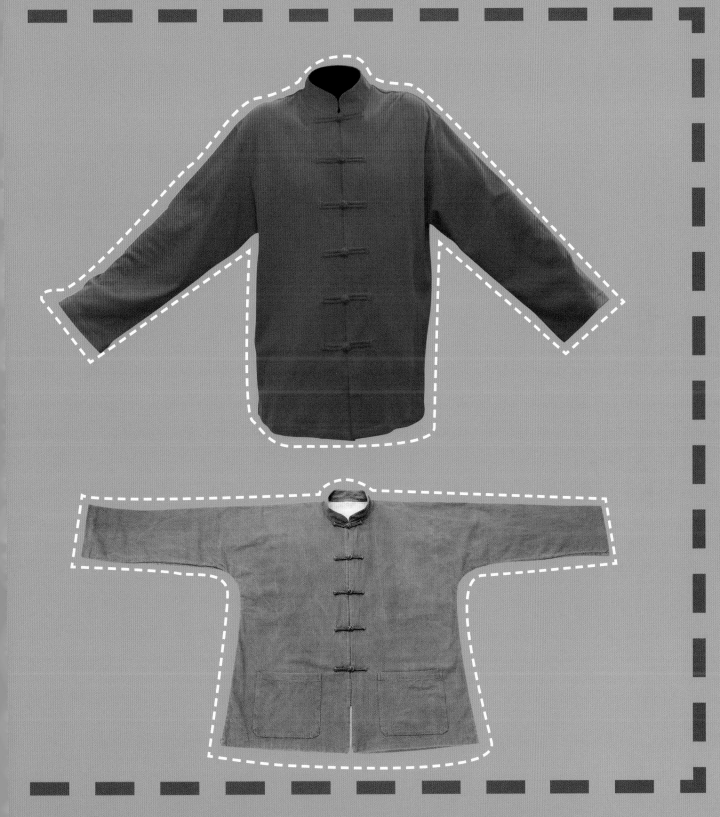

Chang Pao

長袍

Like the *qi pao*, which accentuates beauty of the Chinese woman, the Chinese gown *chang pao* or *cheongsam* was the preferred choice for men for many centuries. This long gown has a clear shape without complicated details. There is usually a slit, which can be closed with hidden buttons, in the middle of the gown, to facilitate mobility while the man is riding a horse. It was regarded as the typical dress of scholars. Although the Chinese gown can rarely be seen nowadays, storytellers still wear this to respect the tradition and create a classic atmosphere.

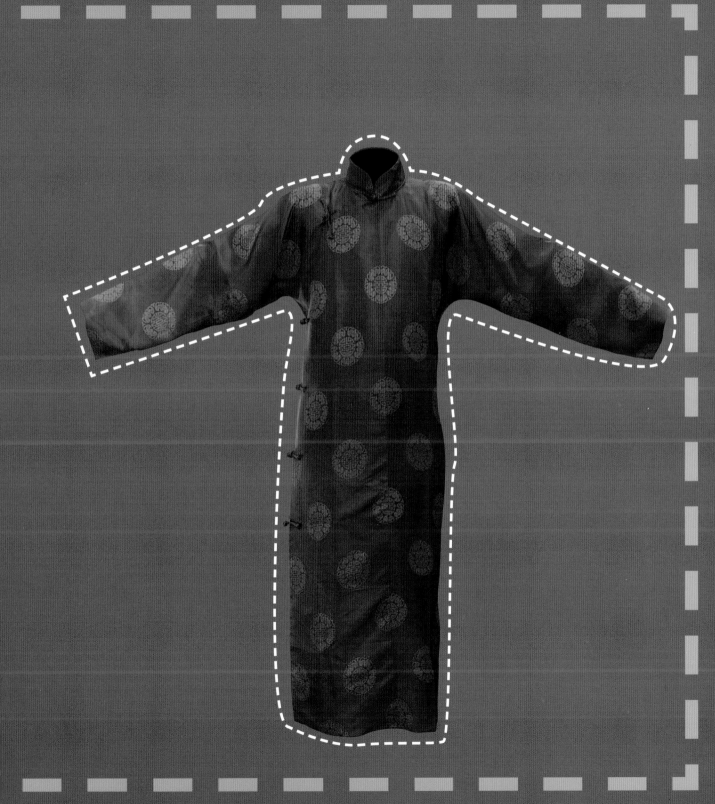

Sun Zhong Shan Suit

中山裝

The *Sun Zhong Shan (Sun Yat-sun)* suit, to some degree, is the symbolic costume for Chinese men, especially during the 20th century. It is named after Dr. Sun Zhong Shan, also known as *Sun Yat-sun*, the Father of the Chinese Revolution who proclaimed in 1911 the new Chinese Republic and served as Provisional President in its early years. Although the suit is mostly confined to museums or historical films nowadays, it has nonetheless impressively represented a movement of the Chinese social evolution.

繡花鞋

Embroidery shoes

20/9/06 Wednesday 2:36 pm

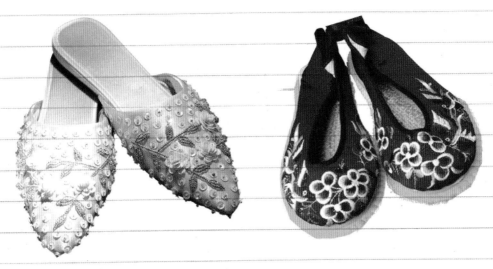

Fabric shoes are made of hemp fibre, silk or brocade. Shoes worn by ladies in red, green or pink are usually embroidered with auspicious design like flowers.

Traditionally, Chinese fabric shoes were a symbol of the working class, commonly worn by ordinary people. The soles of these boots were made from 32 layers of cloth and have since become known as one thousand layered shoes.

帽子

Headgear

Gua pi mao originating from Manchu, was usually worn by Chinese men. The headgear is sewn from six pieces of fabric and looks like gua pi, the skin of watermelons, hence giving it its name. This headgear is a traditional cap for old and young. Typically, it was made of brocade and worn by affluent young men in the Qing Dynasty. It was common to attach a piece of jade in the front panel of the cap.

Silk headgears for boys were embellished with exquisitely colourful embroideries of the Chinese characters *fu* for luck, *lu* for prosperity, *shou* for longevity and *xi* for happiness.

CAP, HAT ?
NO, HEADGEAR.

兒童

children's wear

The set of short sleeved *tang style* pyjamas for a
child is made of indigo print cloth and trimmed
with red silk.

Han Buddhism

佛教

Buddhism formally spread into China in several waves; one important was the Northern Han area during the Han Dynasty, 206 BC - 220 AD.

Burning incense is an old custom passed down from ancient worshiping rituals. When Chinese rendered cults to their Gods and ancestors in the earlier historic times, they usually burned their sacrifices or simply certain plants to create heavy smoke, thus facilitating communication with the spirits through the smoke. This practice has further evolved and survived in the form of burning incense as a popular way of showing respect to the spirits or ancestors. Nowadays, burning incense is the most common way of worshiping spirits. When lighting incense and candles, people worship spirits by bowing down on their knees several times; the more pious kneel down to kowtow and pray silently at the same time.

Buddhist Temple

After Buddhism was introduced into China, temples had an assortment of names like *ci* or *lan ruo*. It was only during the Ming Dynasty, 1368-1644 AD, when the common term *si* (寺), referred to temples throughout the country. The character *si* was originally used to name palaces or mansions of high officials in the early Qin Dynasty and high administrative institutions during the Han Dynasty. Subsequent usage of *si* for Buddhist temples showed the high regard for the religion. The *si* was also laid out according to traditional Chinese palace architecture. There are usually one or several groups of courtyards and halls set on a north-south axis with side rooms flanking symmetrically on each side. Unlike Western churches, most *si* were located remotely.

Gods

※

佛

The Four Heavenly Kings are believed to be the guardians of the world. Heavenly King of the North, Duo Wen, carries a huge umbrella. Whenever he opens his umbrella, the sky over the battlefield turns dark and a cyclonic storm howls, sending sand and rocks whirling about. Heavenly King of the East, Chi Guo, is a helmeted warrior who plays a *pi pa*, a four-stringed Chinese lute. On the battlefield, he plucks the musical instrument and gives his enemy a headache. Heavenly King of the South, Zeng Zhang, has the most furious expression on his face. He holds a magic sword in his hand. When ghosts and monsters dare to step in, he chants an incantation and throws his magic sword up into the sky. Heavenly King of the West, Guang Mu, is represented with a water snake. Once released, the snake mounts the clouds and rides the mists. All of a sudden, this animal spurts out water and disperses his enemy.

Ru Lai Fo, *Sakyamuni*, is the main Buddha in Han Buddhism. It is believed that *Sakyamuni* came from the sun and is the oldest Dhyani Buddha or Meditation Buddha. His rounded statues and human appearance in China is heavily influenced by Chinese culture, especially by the Zen sect and looks very different from original, more mystical images of *Sakyamuni* in other Buddhist regions.

The statues of the heavenly gods who protect the law are usually presented along the aisles of the *Main Buddha Halls* in Buddhist temples. They are called *er shi zhu tian*, referring to the twenty gods protecting the heavenly law.

Guan Yin, *Avalokiteshvara*, is the Bodhisattva of Compassion. Depicted as male in Tibet and India and female in China and East Asia, *Avalokiteshvara*, is believed to have 108 forms. The most powerful form being that of the *Thousand-armed, thousand-eyed Avalokiteshvara. Avalokiteshvara* has great power help and also bless families with a boy.

MONASTIC LIFE

Most Buddhist temples are laid out with gates, halls and courtyards. Their sizes vary according to the importance of the temple and are mainly yellow. They are normally hidden from civilization, situated in quiet areas, on mountains or in deep valleys surrounded by forests.

The entrance to a monastery is called the Shan Men, *mountain gate*, followed by a solemn screen wall to prevent direct peering from the outside. There is a courtyard symmetrically flanked by double-storied structures, the Bell Tower and Drum Tower. The Tian Wang Dian, *hall of heavenly kings*, is the first hall on the main axis. A second courtyard forms the core part of the temple, which includes the main Great Buddha Hall. A huge bronze incense burner, *the ding*, used for religious or ritual ceremonies, is found in front of the Great Buddha Hall for people to burn incense for prayer. Side rooms in this courtyard house other Buddhas and reputed dignitaries. There are two to three courtyards behind, potentially with garden and more halls serving other purposes of meditation, housing sutras, canteen and extremely simple living quarters of the monks.

The traditional large-scale temple, Lin Yin Temple, in the eastern part of China, Hangzhou, is more than 1600 years old. During its heydays, it housed 18 pavilions, 72 halls, 1300 rooms and over 3000 monks.

TAOISM

Taoism is the indigenous religion of China. *Dao* or *Tao*, seeks to be close to nature, meditate in serenity to unite with heaven and spiritual powers that may award immortality to the advanced practice. The true beginning of the Taoist religion started when the influential mystic Zhang Dao Ling, established a new movement called the *The Tao of Five Pecks of Rice*, revering Lao Zi as spiritual leader.

The teachings of Lao Zi, *Lao-tzu*, 1,600-501BC, began as *dao jia*, a school of philosophy. It became a religious tradition *dao jiao* and Lao Zi the key founder of Taoist ideals was revered as a supreme deity. The name Lao Zi simply means *old master*, fitting the ancient philosopher who is believed to have written the book *Dao De Jing*.

The Great Heavenly Jade Emperor 玉皇大帝

The Great Heavenly Jade Emperor, simply called the Jade Emperor, is highly respected in Taoism. He is the emperor of all heavens. The holy birthday of the Jade Emperor falls on the ninth day of the first month of the lunar calendar. On this day, the Chinese worship the Jade Emperor with the *Offering to Heaven* rite, to pray for luck and longevity. All members of the family, after fasting and bathing, burn incense, prostrate, offer food, and recite scriptures. In some places, operas are performed to please the deity.

White Cloud Temple 白雲觀

Bai Yun Guan, White Cloud Temple, the Taoist temple situated in the south of Beijing, is one of the most important Taoist temples in China. It is 1,300 years old and was formally reopened in 1984 for the first time since the 1949 Revolution. Since the establishment of the People's Republic of China in 1949, the practice of Taoism was connected with feudalistic superstition and was more restricted than Buddhism.

The White Cloud Temple is the main temple of the Quan Zhen Taoist sect. According to historical records, Emperor Xuan Zong of the Tang Dynasty had built a temple called Tian Chang Guan to enshrine a stone statue of Lao Zi. Tian Chang Guan was burned down in 1202, but was rebuilt and renamed Tai Ji Palace. It was later damaged during war. Emperor Genghis Khan of the Yuan Dynasty rebuilt the temple and invited Qiu Chang Chun, founder of the Long Men sub-sect under the Quan Zhen sect, to live there in 1224. Qiu died in 1227 and the Emperor renamed the temple Chang Chun Palace in his memory. The temple got its present name in the Ming Dynasty and was rebuilt and repaired several times. Previously, a large fair was held in the temple during the first 20 days of the first lunar month. The Chinese came from far away to venerate the enshrined statues, do business and enjoy themselves.

The Four Dragon Kings 龍王

The four Dragon Kings, in Chinese mythology, are the divine rulers of the *four seas*, each sea corresponds to one of the cardinal directions. Although Dragon Kings appear in their true forms as dragons, they have the ability to shift into human form. The Dragon Kings live in crystal palaces, guarded by *shrimp soldiers* and *crab generals*. Besides ruling over the aquatic life, the Dragon Kings also manipulate clouds and rain. When enraged, they can flood cities. They have been incorporated into the Taoist pantheon from very old legends to symbolize mystic power, but are not among the highest ranking in the hierarchy of worship.

The Dragon King of the Eastern Sea is believed to rule the largest territory. Dragon Kings appear commonly in literature. Detailed descriptions are given of the refinement of their crystal palaces. A Dragon King is one of the main characters in the Chinese literature classic, *Journey to the West*. Numerous temples are dedicated to Dragon Kings in China.

heaven

崇拜天地

Tiantan, the Temple of Heaven

The worship of heaven and earth is important in China. The Chinese believed that heaven is round and earth is square. In most Taoist temples, there is a Hall of the Three Pristine Ones, where the middle position is occupied by the sculpture of the Primeval Lord of Heaven. Taoists, officials and laymen visited temples in the olden days, burned incense and offered sacrifices to him. In Beijing, the Temple of Heaven, which was built during the Ming Dynasty in 1420 A.D, to offer sacrifice to Heaven, includes a park and covers an area of about 2,700,000sqm. As Chinese emperors called themselves The Son of Heaven, they did not dare to build their own dwelling, the Forbidden City larger than one to worship Heaven, hence the Temple of Heaven is much bigger than the Forbidden City. The Temple of Heaven is enclosed with a long wall. Within its walls, the northern part is semicircular symbolizing heaven and the southern part is square symbolizing the earth. So the northern part is higher than the southern part, because the Chinese believed that heaven is bigger than earth. An image of the Temple of Heaven in Beijing shows the only blue-coloured royal dragon symbol found of ancient China.

The Temple of the Earth is located further North. Today it is still quite popular to burn incense in the temples of the Earth Spirit on the first and the fifth day of each month.

trigram

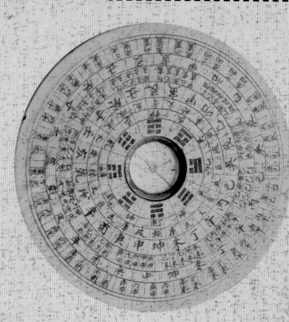

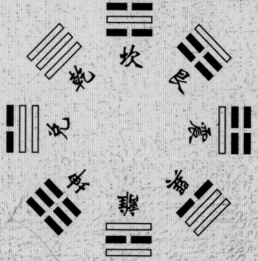

Ba Gua, the Eight Trigram Theory

The *Eight Trigram* theory is older than most Chinese characters, some of which like *shui* (水), the character for water were derived from trigrams. Trigrams were represented by eight sets of three straight lines often arranged in a circle, evolved from the markings on the shell of a tortoise by the legendary Emperor Fu Xi. They are built from unbroken lines representing *yang, the male principle* and broken lines, representing *yin, the female principle*. The arrangement in a circle is important, as it refers to the cyclic changes of nature and is fundamental for the understanding of Chinese philosophy from its earliest beginning. The symbolic value of the trigrams was considered a cosmic secret. *Yi jing, The Book of Changes* from the Zhou Dynasty explains the *Eight Trigrams* as eight simple characters of heaven, marsh, fire, thunder, wind, water, hill and earth, created by ancient sages who carved them on wood, stone and soil. The Chinese believe that two opposing yet complimentary cosmic forces of energies shape the universe and everything in it. They refer to these two energies as *yin* and *yang*. Together, *yin* and *yang* constitute a balanced whole known as *tai ji*. Depicted as a circle, it is an expression to symbolize the all-encompassing completeness, wholeness and all existence. *Tai ji* is the great limit within the unlimited and the bounty that encompasses substance and matter in the universe. The interaction of *yin* and *yang* is reflected by night and day, positive and negative, active and passive, hard and soft, fast and slow, male and female, hot and cold, anger and happiness, and so on. The *yin* and *yang* concept brings about balance and harmony, which in turn brings good fortune.

town god

Cheng Huang, the Temple of the Town God

The Chinese believed that every city had its own protector called Cheng Huang, Town God. There is a Cheng Huang Temple, Temple of the Town God, located in the centre of the Old Town in most cities of China. In Taoist tradition, Cheng Huang was originally a god, who later became an important head and kept his citizens living peacefully and happily. He is the deity who protects the cities and blesses the people, and is in charge of registers in the nether world.

The Chinese held ceremonies and offered sacrifices each year to the Town God. Farmers prayed for rich harvest and businessmen for high income. The Town God had the power to give rain when there was a drought and sunshine when there was a flood. Today, the Chinese still go to Cheng Huang Temple during the festivals.

恭喜發財

God of Fortune

No other god has such a powerful impact on the Chinese way life as the God of Fortune. God of Fortune is the deity of wealth. In Taoist temples, the God of Fortune is often depicted riding a black tiger, with a black and long-bearded face, a rod and treasure in both hands, and wearing an ancient military uniform. He has the image of Marshal Zhao, the Martial Spirit of Wealth, also known as Zhao Gong Ming or Zhao Xuan Tan. Other versions of the God of Fortune, include the image of Bi Gan, Fan Li, Stellar Sovereign Cai Bo and the Star of Prosperity, who along with the Star of Luck and the Star of Longevity, make the Three Stars. Hand crafted sculptures and colourful prints of the God of Fortune are popular across the country. He normally wears fine clothing, hat and shoes, with a white, smiling face fitting of the happy atmosphere of the Lunar New Year, when his images are hung on walls or doors in every family. According to popular custom, on the fifth day of the Lunar New Year, the God of Fortune descends to inspect the world. Hence that morning, the Chinese would set off tons of firecrackers and hire lion dances to entice the God of Fortune to stop by at their house, hoping for a good start and making a big fortune in the coming year. It is said that the God of Fortune was so rich throughout his life that even after his ascension to heaven, he was still in charge of watching over worldly wealth, as well as official posts and ranks. However, the God of Fortune was never incorporated into the traditional pantheon of Taoist immortals.

Ancestors

Ancestor worship ensures the continuity of the memory of the family and reverence for the wisdom of the elders. The ancient practices date back from before 1000 BC. The Chinese prepare paper money, paper gold, paper clothing and all sort of symbolic material goods for the perceived needs of the dead. Popular belief has it that the nether world is similar to earth and ancestors return occasionally to visit relatives. On anniversaries for the dead, the Chinese offer real meals to the spirits of their ancestors in general, with an extra bowl of rice and chopsticks for the person remembered. The living bows to the dead while burning incense and paper money. Ching Ming Festival on the fifth day of the fourth month is the biggest official day for ancestor worship. Similar to All Souls Day, it is the festival for sweeping graves and remembrance. Offerings are burnt on this day. They include traditional joss paper cut into individual squares or rectangles, with a thin piece of square foil glued to its centre or endorsed with a traditional red seal. Contemporary varieties of joss paper include mock bank notes, paper credit cards. Offerings also include paper villas and paper Mercedes-Benz cars.

Joss paper, *xi bo* (锡箔), are sheets of paper that are burned during traditional Chinese festivals or ancestor worship ceremonies. It is traditionally made from coarse bamboo or rice paper and folded by hand into boats to help the souls of the ancestors *cross the river* to rejoin the living. Joss paper also symbolise money that could be used in afterlife. It is thrown to the wind during a funeral procession, left on a grave or burned in ceremonial fires.

The Chinese have invented a wide variety of activities and games. A number of these pastimesarecommonlyengagedthroughout the country. Some popular leisure activities include playing tile or board games like *mah jong*, cards and chess. The Chinese are game to engage companions in these games anywhere and everywhere, even in

public places like alleys, parks, roadside, corridors or any spot shaded from the sun. Games and toys in China are usually manufactured with very simple materials. Popular games are those that require a good measure of strategy or tactical practice to excel.

雜毛毽子
Chinese hacky sack

The Chinese hacky-sack, which looks like a shuttlecock, is a small toy made of cockerel feathers held together with ancient coins at the base. It is a unique indigenous game in China, dating back almost 2,000 years. The basic rule for kicking the hacky-sack is simply to keep it in the air, by kicking it as many times as possible without dropping to the ground. More easily said than done, it requires excellent coordination and balance, and hacky-sack fans have complicated the game more by including moves like twists and turns, combined with a range of kicking techniques. Besides kicking by foot and knee; the head, forehead, shoulder, and back also are allowed to be used to keep the shuttlecock moving. Hacky-sack kicking, practiced individually or in groups, is not just a game, but also a healthy exercise for raising legs, moving the body and jumping. This activity, which challenges balance and reaction as well, does not require much space, so it can be practiced anywhere and anytime.

陀螺
Top

The Chinese top is a spinning toy, which has a sharp point of axis that touches and whirl on the ground. The common whipping top is made of wood with a flat round top and a pointed bottom. An iron nail on the pointed side reinforces the top. A string is wound up around the body of the top together with an ancient coin or a flattened bottle top. The top is thrown out and the line pulled back, whipping the top into a whirling motion on the ground. Worked by a skilful player, the top spins so fast that the colours would fuse harmoniously and the humming sound will become louder. The experts are even able to choreograph the spinning motions of the tops throughout the game.

中國溜溜球
Diabolo

The diabolo or Chinese yo-yo is a juggling prop consisting of a spool, which is whirled and tossed on a string tied to two sticks held one in each hand. It is also called *pull-bell* because of its bell-like shape. There are two forms of diabolo - the single-bell and the double-bell. For the beginner, it is tricky to balance the control on the two sticks while creating the right thrust, as the diabolo moves quickly on the string. The double-bell looks like two wheels on an axis and is easier to start with. With skilful precision, the diabolo is spun, thrown and twisted around the body of the expert player. The player and his diabolo should be like two beings linked together in a dancing mode, building a crescendo of dramatic choreography and skilful manipulation.

風車
Paper windmill

Chinese paper windmills are made of light, round wheels with several coloured blades set at an angle, mounted on sticks or bamboo handles. The Chinese believe the round shape of the windmill would drive away evil and keep good fortune rolling in. In fact, more luck will be brought in with more windmills piled up or if they turn more quickly.

In Chinese *feng shui*, wind and water is believed to change in turns. During Chinese New Year, new paper windmills bring good luck for the New Year. Especially in the northern and southern parts of China, in major cities like Beijing and Hong Kong, there are all kinds of windmill for sale at the New Year temple fairs.

風箏
Kite

The whistle of kites flying high overhead sounded like the *zheng*, the Chinese zither, an ancient musical instrument, such that although not all kites made such a sound, the name of *feng zheng, wind zither*, has stuck and spread from generation to generation. *Feng zheng* came in an assortment of forms and colours like fish and butterflies and are sold at the gates of most suburban parks.

彈弓
Slingshot

The *dan gong* or slingshot, used to be a good tool for catching birds. The body is simply fashioned from a sturdy y-shaped twig, with rubber band or any elastic string looped between the branches. Small stones are used as bullets, shot from the sling pad in the middle of the elastic loop.

Kaleidoscope

Kaleidoscopes were tributes to the emperor and noblemen during late Qing Dynasty when it first appeared in China, probably imported from the West. Although it started out as a very exclusive and novel toy in its early days, the kaleidoscope was popularised very quickly. Cheap and colourful imitations of this elite toy of bygone days now swamp the market as accessible objects of everyone. They are usually multi-coloured in plastic and have reached out to all parts of the world.

Chinese chess

Xiang qi, Chinese chess is one of the most popular board game in the world. Chinese chess draws its particular historic background from a famous battle in ancient China 2,200 years ago, when two opposite kingdoms of Chu and Han went to war. They form two opposite camps on the chessboard, centrally divided by River Chu dating from that time. Similar to the international chess, *xiang qi* is a mind exercise only much faster. The movement of the pieces tend to be more fluid and the positions more open. Chinese chess is a more tactical game than a strategic one. There is no careful build-up of pawn structures and the major pieces come into play immediately. Draws are rare.

Basic Rules

Player takes alternate turns. At each turn, a player must make a single move with a single piece. If a piece ends its move on a point occupied by an enemy piece, that piece is captured and permanently removed from play. The objective of the game is to capture the general of the enemy. The game is won as soon as checkmate, where one player can make no move to prevent the capture of his general. Stalemate, where one player has no legal move but is not in check, is a win for the last player to move. It is illegal to move into check, which is a move that exposes your general to immediate capture. It is also illegal to avoid defeat or attempt to force a draw by repeating the same series of moves over and over. In particular, perpetual check is not allowed, and the onus is on the attacker to vary his move.

The Board

Traditional Chinese chessboard and most other Chinese game boards are hardly any boards at all. Usually of soft or light materials like paper or textile, they are printed with all the relevant markings. The chessboards are at best mounted on a piece of cardboard, but normally easy to wrap up and mobile for transport to any other spot.

The Pieces

Each player has 16 pieces, a general (King), two mandarins (assistants), two elephants (ministers), two horses, two chariots (rooks), two cannons and five soldiers (pawns). In all cases except that of the cannon, pieces move the same way when capturing or not.

Popularity of the Game

While many other games, including mah jong and some card games, were strictly forbidden during the Cultural Revolution in mainland China, and were not seen in the public realm for more than ten years, Chinese chess has enjoyed undivided popularity during those days and was and still is widely played in open air places.

Animal Chess

Dou shou qi, animal chess used to be a very popular board game in China. It is a cross between Stratego and Chinese Chess. Like all great board games, *dou shou qi* is easy to learn, but hard to master. The existence of terrain including river, in which no animal can swim except the rat and pits, which reverse the usual rule that big animals capture smaller ones, adds a nice strategic layer to the game. In this two-player game, animals have different ranks and abilities. Each animal can move one step at a time on the board and capture animals that are smaller than they are. In a twist, the rat, the smallest can defeat the largest, the elephant, as well as swim across the river. The objective of the game is to place an animal in the den of the opponent. Each animal can only move one step at a time, except lions and tigers, which can leap in one step across the river or over land bridges.

Aeroplane Game

Fei xing qi, aeroplane game, is a very popular children's board game in China, resembling to Ludo in many ways. With a maximum of four-players, each player controls four aeroplanes of a singular colour around the board. In general, the players move the pieces according to the number decided by the dice. Its simple rule and numerous variable factors include shortcuts, jumping and kicking out the pieces of other players, have added great interest to this game. The player whose four pieces arrive at the destination first wins.

War Game

Jun qi, the war game is a modern strategic game, requiring great skill and deduction. It is a battle between the military ranks of two players. A third person is necessary to act as a referee for this game. The main idea of *jun qi* is that players can only see their own pieces, but not that of their opponent, so they do not know what move the opponent has made. Players rely on partial information that allows them to deduce where the opponent set his pieces. The referee judges on which pieces are captured. Players move in turns, just as in normal chess. With each turn, a player attempts a move. When a piece meets another piece, the referee will judge and announce whose piece could move, while the lesser rank is captured. At the end, the one who captures the army flag of the opponent wins, regardless of number of pieces lost. Little wonder why this game was very popular during the cultural revolution.

麻將 Mah jong

Ma jiang or *mah jong* is a classic Chinese game for four. It is the most widespread pastime of the Chinese New Year celebrations and in general, a typical time killer for well-to-do ladies of the Chinese society, often played with money. There are 144 tiles in a set of *mah jong*. It consists of 36 tiles in the Bamboo suite (Sow), 36 in the Circle suite (Pin), 36 in the Character suite (Wan), 16 Wind tiles, 12 Dragon tiles and 8 bonus tiles (4 Flowers and 4 Season). Each of the four players sits at one of the points of the compass - North, South, East, and West. The tiles are shuffled around, facing down, then drawn and arranged in stacks to later form a wall. The first dealer represents East and it is his job to throw the dice to break the wall. After dealing according to certain rules, each player ends up with 13 cards, after which they begin the discarding and hoarding process. The object of the game is to get triples, *peng*, quadruples, *gang*, or sequences of three in the same suit *hu pai*. When you have 4 of the above and a pair in your hand, a total of 14 tiles, you have mah jong and have won the hand.

圍棋 Go

Wei qi or *go* is a strategic board game originating from ancient China between 2000 BC and 200 BC. The game involves two players who alternate black and white stones on a checkerboard of 19 vertical lines by 19 horizontal lines. As there are 180 white stones and 181 black ones, black moves first. Stones must have leave *liberties*, empty adjacent points, on the board. Stones connected by lines are called chains and share *liberties*. When the opponent surrounds a stone or a chain of stones, it has no more *liberties*, and is captured and removed from the board. A stone cannot be played on a particular point, if doing so would recreate the board position as his previous turn. A player may pass instead his turn for placing a stone. When both players pass consecutively, the game ends and scored. A score is given for the number of empty points enclosed by the stones of a player, plus the number of points occupied by his stones. The player with the higher score wins.

 玩鳥 Raising Birds

Raising birds is a popular leisure activity in China. In the past, raising birds was a luxurious amusement for the rich, but today it is a more common recreation for retirees. In the mornings, bird fanatics stroll with their caged birds in parks, and get together with other bird fans to exchange experiences of rearing and training their prized birds. A well-trained bird could obey the directive of its owner and perform simple tricks. In China, when old folks gather at the teahouse and stop for a drink, they would place their birdcages in a row in front of the gate of the house, ensuring a very melodious concert.

A birdcage is usually made of bamboo. In the past, an exquisite birdcage was pricey, hence raising birds was a pastime only the rich could afford.

 鬥蟋蟀 Cricket fights

Cricket fight is an original form of competition from ancient China, popular since the Song Dynasty. It was a simple form of entertainment enjoyed by common people. When the cricket fight begins, two crickets are put on a special arena, covered with a transparent net so that the fight can be observed. Royal courts used to organise a lot of these matches. The innate aggression of male crickets against other male crickets is exercised. The cricket attempts to pluck the legs or feelers of its opponent. Crickets are trained not only how to attack but also other formats of combat. It is estimated that a well-trained cricket can apply about 20 methods of attack. Cricket boxes, in which the crickets were transported in were genuine masterpieces of art usually made of bamboo. Before the fight, the crickets are kept in the boxes at high temperature, by covering the walls with knitted wool, thick felt or thick cloth. During the fight, the crickets are stroked with special brushes, made of mouse hair. A fight usually lasts about 15 minutes. Defeated crickets, usually without legs and feelers, are usually thrown away. Exceptionally brave crickets are buried with full honour. A chorus of the crickets precedes the fight. The sounds they produce are made more resonant when special brass vibrators, coiled at one end are put into the boxes. The coil intensifies the sound and gives it an even more musical character.

 **Fireworks**

Setting off fireworks is an important custom for the Chinese. It is used to expresses happiness during joyful occasions like weddings or store openings and promotes auspiciousness during Chinese New Year celebrations. The history of fireworks can be traced back more than 2,000 years. In ancient times, firecrackers were simply burnt bamboo sticks, which gave its name *pao zhu*, cracking bamboo. The Chinese used firecrackers, which made explosive sounds, to drive away ghosts, or evil spirits who were scared of sound and light. Among which *nian* or year, was a beast, which appeared yearly, hence the origin of traditions to set off fireworks during the Chinese New Year. Further improvements of fireworks came with technical developments. Colourful and luminescent materials are added to gunpowder to create complex fireworks that form a splendid show when they explode in the sky.

 **Firecackers**

Soon after the invention of gunpowder in China, it was filled into bamboo tubes to produce an enormous sound. The bamboo tubes were eventually replaced with paper cartons, usually wrapped in red. The smaller firecrackers were assembled in chains, which would set off like machine-guns, a continuous chain of festivity sounds.

Da di hong, are strings of hundreds or thousands of small firecrackers, which are popular firecrackers in China. After they are set off with their machine-gun like noise, their burnt scraps would drop on the ground, leaving red paper scraps, which symbolizes joy.

Folklore & Handicraft

民俗文化和小玩意

Chinese folk custom is tightly linked with numerous traditional festivals and legendary tales. Gifted craftsmen have created all kinds of articles to embellish the lives of common folk, many of which can be considered unique and artistic treasures. The fabric tiger is a popular form of folk art in the northern part of China. The Chinese

treat the tiger as a symbol to protect wealth and ward off evil. Especially during the festivals of Dragon Boat, Spring and Mid Autumn. The tiger usually has a big head with big eyes, big mouth and big tail as a sign of courage and power.

Fan

The fan is symbolic of China and the Far East in general. The history of the making of traditional fans can be traced back to the Western Han Dynasty, 206 BC-23 AD. Fans are be made of exquisite materials, such as ivory, sandalwood, feathers, paper, silk, bamboo, hawksbill tortoise shells, as well as simple palm leaves. The varieties of fans include palace fans, folding fans, black paper fans, feather fans, palm-leaf fans, *gong* fans, ivory fans as well as sandalwood fans. In ancient times, fans were widely used to keep cool and to ward off strong sunlight and dust. But today, it is predominantly a decorative accessory, still appreciated for its artistic value, especially when painted by well-known artists with paintings, poetry, calligraphy or prints of seals. Some of them are even decorated with ivory, jade or pearl. The outlines of covering paintings on fans may be round or shaped like a phoenix's tail, kidney, ancient bell, or crab-apple blossom.

畫蛋

Painted egg-shell

Eggshell painting is traditional folk art, which has nothing to do with Easter. It is a decorative art form where artists draw pictures and do light paintings on the eggshell of chicken or goose, solely for the purposes of pleasing the eye. A variety of subjects are drawn, all of them charming.

Moulding human figurines and animals from coloured clay or glutinous rice flour is a popular art form both in urban and rural areas in China. Chinese dough sculptures date back to the Han Dynasty, 206 BC-220 AD. The perfect dough is made in three steps. First, honey, lard, powdered sugar and refined powder are dissolved in boiling water, before all is mixed with flour. Edible pigments are added to

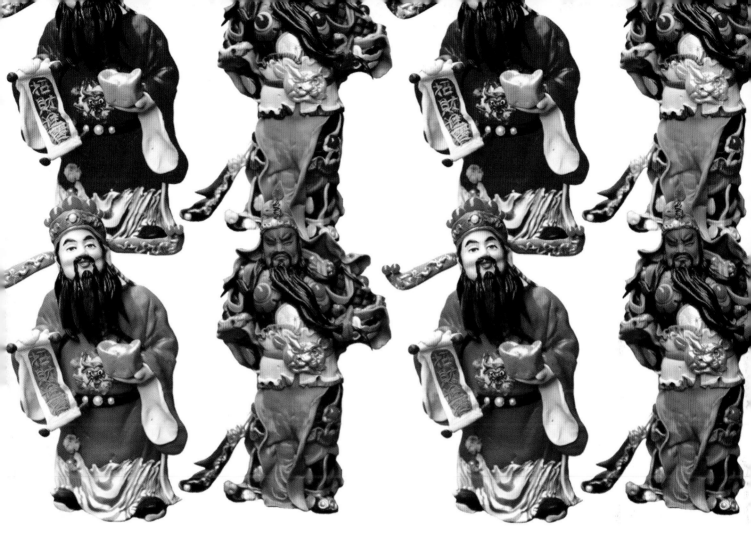

泥塑

Chinese dough sculptures

form pastes of different colours. Next, the pastes are steamed for two or three minutes. Care is taken not to over-cook them, or they would become lustreless. Lastly, oil is smeared onto the dough with a brush to make it gleam. With well-prepared dough, accomplished dough artists can produce a vivid dough sculpture with amazing speed using simple tools like scissors, kitchen knife and combs. Dough sculptures from the Yellow River Valley region are simple, crude, unconstrained and profound, while those from the Yangtze River Valley region delicate, exquisite and polished.

皮影戲

Shadow Play

Pi ying xi, shadow play is an art form still alive today in Huanxian County of Gansu Province, where external cultural influence is limited due to its remoteness. Huanxian County now has more than 90 shadow play groups, all of which are made up of farmers. Shadow play is a kind of drama in which silhouettes made of hard paper and hide are projected onto a white screen. It was first developed almost 1,000 years ago. While shadow play originated from Han Dynasty, it was popularised during the Song Dynasty, 960-1279 AD. In the 13th century, it spread to other countries of Asia and North Africa, and eventually to Europe in the 17th century. The performer manipulates the characters behind the screen while singing the libretto that tells the story. The shadow puppets walked, danced, and performed various kinds of movements by strings connected to the joints, to the accompaniment of music and songs.

草編
Wheatshaft Weave

Wheat shaft weave, is the general name given to daily articles and ornaments woven from wheat shaft. Woven daily appliances include grass hats, plates and cushions. Some ornaments are for enjoyment or decoration purpose only like these dolls, which are popular handicraft items. Wheat shafts are woven into plaits and the plaits are chained together. All the wheat producing areas in the northern parts of China have developed such weaving techniques.

篆刻
Seal Carving

The seal has for many centuries been a symbol of power for the Chinese. The xi or the seal of the emperor gave him authority over his subjects. His government at different levels all issued orders endorsed with official seals. The seal stood for the different levels of government and their corresponding powers. The art of seal engraving or carving can be traced back more than 3,000 years to the Yin Dynasty. It developed rapidly during the Qin Dynasty, 221-207 BC, when people engraved their names on utensils to claim ownership. Today, seals are still widely used and the art of seal carving has become more popular.

A master seal engraver must write in different styles of Chinese scripts and arrange all the characters in a perfect balance. A perfect seal is very much determined by the speed of the engraver and strength of his wrist and finger movements, as well as the particular tool he uses. Stone is the most widely used material, although the engraver should familiarise with other materials like jade, gold, brass and wood, so that he may apply his tool with the right strength and rhythm.

鼻煙壺
Snuff Bottle

The Chinese initially used phials to hold snuff, a powdered tobacco that is sniffed up the nostril rather than smoked. Assorted materials and craftworks were used to improve snuff bottles. The making of snuff bottles in China has a history of over 400 years. Apart from practical usage, snuff bottles were also regarded as precious gifts to international contacts of the Qing Dynasty. Snuff bottles made from precious materials reflected the status of their owners. The bottles were created into exquisite snuff bottles by skilful handicraftsmen out of an assortment of materials from precious stones, minerals, metals, glass, porcelain, sometimes even amber, to the most mundane materials, such as the pits of fruits, roots and stems of plants. During the Qing Dynasty many famous snuff bottle masters and workshops developed. Today, there is also a Snuff Bottle Association in China that devotes its time to promoting and developing this traditional handicraft.

中國花瓶

Chinese Vase

Traditional Chinese vases were made of porcelain, a fine material created in China. Chinese exports of porcelain in the 17th and 18th centuries were held in high esteem in Europe, so much so that porcelain became synonymous with China. Porcelain has properties of low permeability, high strength, hardness, gloss, durability, whiteness, translucence, resonance, brittleness, high resistance to the passage of electricity, high resistance to thermal shock and high elasticity. It is used to make wares for the table and kitchen, sanitary ware, decorative sculptures and objects of fine art.

景泰藍

Cloisonné

Cloisonné is also known as enamelware. To the Chinese, this art form is typically called the Blue of Jing Tai. During the reign of Jing Tai, 1450-1456, in the Ming Dynasty, craftsmen prevalently adopted the navy-blue glaze as the dominant colour for enamelling and creating brilliant designs. The capital Beijing is the cradle of cloisonné and is proud of its 500-year history. In Beijing, most shops sell cloisonné pieces, as big as screens, tables and chairs, to articles as small as chopsticks, earrings, candy boxes, toothpick holders and smoking tools. This cloisonné peacock has a remarkably realistic expression and posture. The tail of the bird can be taken apart, so as to transport it conveniently. The cloisonné technique is a combination of copper and porcelain craftsmanship, as well as the Chinese traditional carving. The procedure of making cloisonné is quite elaborate and sophisticated. First, soft copper is hammered and stretched to shape the cloisonné body. Next, copper wire strips are added onto the copper body to form various patterns. This process is professionally called filigree soldering. Then the compartments are filled separately with enamel glaze in different colours. Lastly, the work is fired, polished and gilded to achieve the final delicate article.

Jade

Jade is the collective name for most precious stones in China. Jade carving constitutes an important part of Chinese arts and crafts. The Chinese proverb claims gold has a price, but jade is priceless. Jade ware is often described as *worth a string of towns*. During the New Stone Age, Neolithic people chose jade purely for its hardness, making it good for making tools and fighting weapons. As time went by, people gradually appreciated the beauty of the stone, which after carving and polishing turns into things not only useful, but also nice to look at and cool to touch. Today, jade carving still remains a handicraft. As raw materials get more and more scarce, the price of jade ware will always be on the upward trend.

木雕
Wood Carving

Decorative woodcarvings in China originated from the Han Dynasties and flourished during the Ming and Qing Dynasties with intricate carvings and elegant forms. The carvings have obtained everlasting fame and are classics of national folk woodcarving. Wooden root carvings are fashioned from natural root with artistic skill. Sculptors carve many different types of roots according to their natural shapes to create man-made sculptures.

小手工藝品
Handicraft

As a kind of national folkloristic handicraft, the Chinese knot technique specialises in making articles from a single piece of string or rope. Most of these objects are considered to be decorative pieces or greeting gifts. Having a long history dating back to ancient times, the majority of the Chinese knots appear in bright red. To the Chinese, the knot has the meaning of reunion, which in turn reminds one of luck, so the Chinese knot is usually hung to express good wishes for happiness, fortune and wealth. The knot can either be single or a combination of several knots accompanied with auspicious ornaments made of different materials, and is named according to its specific form and profound cultural meaning. Double happiness, luck, security, peace and longevity are the most typical examples.

Nowadays, the Chinese knot is applied to variety of products, so as to fit in with the needs of modern living. Auspicious room decorations, small objects for the car and knitting clothing adornments are commonly seen these days.